Handbooks
FOR
Humans

Volume 1

Learn to Manage
Your Attitudes in
all Your Relationships

Grace Anne Stevens

Graceful Change Press • Lexington

Handbooks for Humans; Volume 1
Learn to Manage Your Attitudes in All Your Relationships

© 2018 Grace Anne Stevens

Graceful Change Press

Kindle Edition, 2018

ISBN 978-0-986300356

No part of this publication may be reproduced, stored in a retrieval system, or transmitted, in any form or by any means, electronic, mechanical, photocopying, recording, or otherwise, without the written prior permission of the author.

Contact:
Grace Stevens
(781) 789-6103
gas333@verizon.net
www.graceannestevens.com

Printed in the United States of America

Contents

My Attitude Is Gratitude 1

How to Use This Handbook for Humans 7

How to Be Human Guidelines 9

The Power of Sharing 203

More Guideline Reflections 209

Books by Grace Anne Stevens 213

About the Author 215

This book is dedicated to each of you who are willing to participate and work at being a better human being.

My Attitude Is Gratitude

The idea of creating Handbooks for Humans has been floating around my mind for the past few years. As I am now entrenched in my eighth decade, I look back on my own evolution in relationships, careers, and mostly my own sense of being.

I have read many self-help books during this journey, and a few have helped me on my journey in different ways. I suspect that you also may be able to make a similar statement reflecting on your own journey. What I have learned so far, or perhaps what I have learned to believe so far, is that almost all of our answers are inside of us, but we are never properly taught how to go inside and access them.

My own experience with reading self-help books, often left me overwhelmed, sometimes drained, and quite often confused. So many words, so many ideas that seemed to be interrelated, it was a good deal of work for me to determine what my next steps could and should be. Sadly, this effort sometimes dissipated, and nothing much changed for me.

Over the past few years, as I began my writing and speaking careers, I began to realize how one can carry powerful messages in just a few words if they were presented in the right way.

You can make people feel, or think, or review their beliefs and their experiences with both statements and questions.

I started to think that perhaps a book of these "words" coupled with a structure to work with how the words landed on your feelings, thoughts, beliefs, and experiences, just might be a new simplified but powerful self-help book.

I have learned that our attitudes are really the intersection of our feelings, our thoughts, our beliefs and our experiences. Our attitudes control all of our interactions in the world.

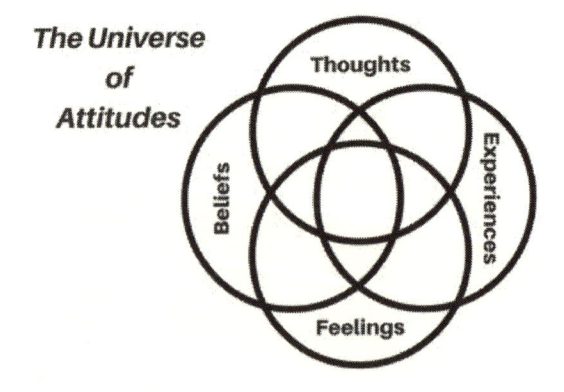

The Universe of Attitudes

Thoughts • Beliefs • Experiences • Feelings

Human interactions are controlled by our attitudes.

Attitudes are a constant balance of thoughts, feelings, beliefs, and experience.

They can change without notice.

If you are willing to explore your attitudes to the guidelines in *Handbooks for Humans: Volume 1*, you might be surprised at what you learn about yourself. I suggest you share your findings and experiences with others too.

For me what I have learned is that my attitude is gratitude.

Grace Anne Stevens
July 2018

Physics teaches us that energy is the ability to do work.

Being human requires work.

Find your energy.

How to Use This Handbook for Humans

There are a number of ways that a reader can use this book.

Good:

Read all the guideline in the book in a single quick sitting. This will only take you a few minutes. Put the book aside and wait.

Better:

Read all the guidelines first.

If you are willing to spend some effort, you will recognize that for each guideline you read, something just may come up for you. It may be a thought with or without some judgment or a feeling with varying levels of emotional triggering. Some people have commented that the guideline might even have them questioning their own beliefs and would rather discuss whether they agree with it or not. Some people might even recognize an experience they have had that reflects on the guideline. Some may have multiple but different experiences with a single guideline.

There are no incorrect responses for any of these. If you are willing to articulate, to your best ability, your thoughts, feelings, beliefs, and experiences, you just may find some new understandings of how you operate as a human being.

Your reflections can be an even more powerful experience if you are working with others and sharing your discoveries.

Review and Repeat

Return to the Handbook when a life event occurs that is referenced by one of the guidelines and make a note of the experience.

Have any of your thoughts, feelings, or beliefs changed?

Share it. Humans share!

Your Way

That's totally up to you by being human. There is no wrong way to read, use, or experience this book.

How to Be Human Guidelines

If you are reading this,

there is a good chance that

you are human.

My thoughts

My feelings

My beliefs

My experience

Humans come in many sizes,

shapes, colors,

and

genders.

They are all still human.

My thoughts

My feelings

My beliefs

My experience

as a human,

you are able.

But

are you willing?

are you ready

to put yourself into self-help?

My thoughts

My feelings

My beliefs

My experience

We are all the same.

My thoughts

My feelings

My beliefs

My experience

Each of us is unique.

My thoughts

My feelings

My beliefs

My experience

Being unique is what

makes us human.

My thoughts

My feelings

My beliefs

My experience

Humans always have many identities.

Balancing them may be difficult work

and

often confusing.

My thoughts

My feelings

My beliefs

My experience

As humans are each unique,

each has unique gifts.

Find,

nurture,

and

share

yours.

My thoughts

My feelings

My beliefs

My experience

It is OK

if you only fit

in a small box.

Remember,

each of us

is unique.

My thoughts

My feelings

My beliefs

My experience

You will make mistakes.

My thoughts

My feelings

My beliefs

My experience

You may make the same mistakes

over again.

My thoughts

My feelings

My beliefs

My experience

Do not count or keep score of

your mistakes

or those of others.

My thoughts

My feelings

My beliefs

My experience

admitting your mistakes is a

high form

of

being human.

My thoughts

My feelings

My beliefs

My experience

anyone can be your teacher,

if you let them.

My thoughts

My feelings

My beliefs

My experience

Acceptance must precede understanding.

Understanding may lead to knowing.

Knowing is never complete.

My thoughts

My feelings

My beliefs

My experience

What you know

is

what you know

so far.

It can change at

any time,

and does.

My thoughts

My feelings

My beliefs

My experience

Almost all animals have perception.

All humans have perspective.

Using both correctly must be learned.

My thoughts

My feelings

My beliefs

My experience

Even though each human is

unique,

they are all connected.

My thoughts

My feelings

My beliefs

My experience

Connections will often

surprise you.

My thoughts

My feelings

My beliefs

My experience

Make as many connections

as you can.

My thoughts

My feelings

My beliefs

My experience

No human can be alone,

and still be human.

My thoughts

My feelings

My beliefs

My experience

Even when you feel alone,

you really are not.

But getting out there is

up to you.

My thoughts

My feelings

My beliefs

My experience

Loving yourself

is necessary,

before

you can love

another.

My thoughts

My feelings

My beliefs

My experience

Remember to love yourself.

It is human.

My thoughts

My feelings

My beliefs

My experience

Do the people you love, know it?

If not, why?

My thoughts

My feelings

My beliefs

My experience

Most people ignore

the first word in the phrase:

Growing old.

Try not to be most people.

My thoughts

My feelings

My beliefs

My experience

Value your values.

My thoughts

My feelings

My beliefs

My experience

Respect

the

values

of

others.

This may be challenging

for most humans.

At least, try.

My thoughts

My feelings

My beliefs

My experience

Celebrate the child in you.

Often.

My thoughts

My feelings

My beliefs

My experience

Make time to play.

My thoughts

My feelings

My beliefs

My experience

Say yes,

Even when it seems hard.

My thoughts

My feelings

My beliefs

My experience

We must be in relationships.

My thoughts

My feelings

My beliefs

My experience

Relationships

are often

hard

and

require constant

work.

My thoughts

My feelings

My beliefs

My experience

The only thing we get to control...

is...

what we choose to give away

to others.

My thoughts

My feelings

My beliefs

My experience

Humans

cannot

read minds.

Sadly,

some think

they can.

My thoughts

My feelings

My beliefs

My experience

Attitudes control

human interactions.

Attitudes are a constant balance

of thoughts, feelings, beliefs, and

experiences.

They can change without notice.

My thoughts

My feelings

My beliefs

My experience

Language is what has allowed humans to create civilizations.

Yet, words cannot always express our thoughts and feelings.

My thoughts

My feelings

My beliefs

My experience

Words

can build us up

or

tear us down.

This can be done on purpose or

by accident.

Correct when necessary.

My thoughts

My feelings

My beliefs

My experience

Humans can tell stories.

Humans can listen to stories.

Some humans do both,
some only one, and some neither.

How does your choice
express your humanity?

My thoughts

My feelings

My beliefs

My experience

Share mealtime

with others and talk,

often.

My thoughts

My feelings

My beliefs

My experience

Humans

require

hugs.

Sometimes we forget

this is never outgrown.

My thoughts

My feelings

My beliefs

My experience

Humans can learn when good enough is good enough,

and when it's not!

Sometimes they get it wrong.

My thoughts

My feelings

My beliefs

My experience

Humans are a blank canvas.

You paint your life in layers.

Create your masterpiece.

My thoughts

My feelings

My beliefs

My experience

There is no

single way

to

be

human.

My thoughts

My feelings

My beliefs

My experience

at some point,

cuddles are more important than climaxes.

They last longer and are shared.

My thoughts

My feelings

My beliefs

My experience

Choose wisely.

My thoughts

My feelings

My beliefs

My experience

It does not matter who wins,

if you have tried your best.

They teach this in Little League.

So many of us forget it.

My thoughts

My feelings

My beliefs

My experience

Happiness
only comes
from inside
of you.

Go inside, let it out.

My thoughts

My feelings

My beliefs

My experience

Sometimes,

it is

OK

to be

silly.

My thoughts

My feelings

My beliefs

My experience

Wants and needs

are often

hard

to tell

apart.

My thoughts

My feelings

My beliefs

My experience

Our work as humans

is to separate

our

wants and needs.

My thoughts

My feelings

My beliefs

My experience

Do you really want

the things

you say

you want?

My thoughts

My feelings

My beliefs

My experience

Do you really need

the things

you say

you need?

My thoughts

My feelings

My beliefs

My experience

The old song tells us
"You Can't Always Get
What You Want."

That is true, but you can learn
to want what you have.

Sometimes it is hard to learn this.

My thoughts

My feelings

My beliefs

My experience

If you have many toys

when you die,

you leave work for

your survivors.

It is your choice.

My thoughts

My feelings

My beliefs

My experience

Listen more.

My thoughts

My feelings

My beliefs

My experience

Don't interrupt.

My thoughts

My feelings

My beliefs

My experience

ask for help.

My thoughts

My feelings

My beliefs

My experience

Smile.

Repeat.

My thoughts

My feelings

My beliefs

My experience

Wander

with

wonder.

Only humans use these together.

Try it.

My thoughts

My feelings

My beliefs

My experience

If you get stuck,

and you will,

you are the only one

who can completely

unstick yourself.

Getting help is human.

My thoughts

My feelings

My beliefs

My experience

Read aloud

to someone.

Often.

My thoughts

My feelings

My beliefs

My experience

No one

is

perfect.

Wanting perfection

gets in the way of

being human.

My thoughts

My feelings

My beliefs

My experience

Very few, if any humans can do it all.

That's OK.

You are only human.

My thoughts

My feelings

My beliefs

My experience

Learning is the first step in being human.

Teaching is the second step.

Learning from those you have taught is the third and perhaps most important step.

Never stop learning.

My thoughts

My feelings

My beliefs

My experience

Reach for the sky.

It is

unlimited.

My thoughts

My feelings

My beliefs

My experience

Wisdom

is

knowledge

plus

experience.

My thoughts

My feelings

My beliefs

My experience

Sometimes,

we ignore

the wisdom

of others.

My thoughts

My feelings

My beliefs

My experience

Sometimes,

others ignore

our wisdom.

My thoughts

My feelings

My beliefs

My experience

Share your wisdom,

even if it is not used.

Use the wisdom

shared with you.

My thoughts

My feelings

My beliefs

My experience

Watch the sun rise from a boat on the water.

My thoughts

My feelings

My beliefs

My experience

Hold a

newborn

baby.

Smell

it's head.

Then you will understand!

My thoughts

My feelings

My beliefs

My experience

You are the only one

who knows your truth.

Living it is being

human.

My thoughts

My feelings

My beliefs

My experience

Be there

for someone.

Over and over.

My thoughts

My feelings

My beliefs

My experience

At some point in your life,

train a dog.

Dogs are not human, but

they are close.

My thoughts

My feelings

My beliefs

My experience

Certainty

often blocks

possibility.

Use with caution.

My thoughts

My feelings

My beliefs

My experience

all things change.

People too!

There is nothing

you can do about it.

My thoughts

My feelings

My beliefs

My experience

Sometimes,

it is easier to change,

than to explain why you did.

It may be harder for those who know you.

Find the words to explain.

My thoughts

My feelings

My beliefs

My experience

If you forget that

change is constant,

you may end up

more disappointed

than is necessary.

My thoughts

My feelings

My beliefs

My experience

Humans often

run with the pack.

This is good.

Remember to

STAND

OUT

ALONE.

My thoughts

My feelings

My beliefs

My experience

Learn from the birds.

Teach your children to fly.

Celebrate

when they leave the nest.

My thoughts

My feelings

My beliefs

My experience

They will return

and

celebrate you!

My thoughts

My feelings

My beliefs

My experience

Memories are like time traveling.

Keep making new ones,

or you can get lost in the past.

My thoughts

My feelings

My beliefs

My experience

It is OK to

wear your heart

on your sleeve.

Then be sure to wear

a clean shirt.

My thoughts

My feelings

My beliefs

My experience

One of the hardest tasks in being human

is knowing

when to lead

or

when to follow.

You must do both.

My thoughts

My feelings

My beliefs

My experience

Resilience is based on

the stories you tell yourself.

Bad things happen.

You can choose the story.

My thoughts

My feelings

My beliefs

My experience

Hold someone

when

they cry.

My thoughts

My feelings

My beliefs

My experience

Find someone to hold you when you cry.

(Repeat as necessary.)

My thoughts

My feelings

My beliefs

My experience

SHARE.

In many ways,

That's how humans connect.

My thoughts

My feelings

My beliefs

My experience

If you have reached the top of
your selected pyramid,
through hard work, luck, or grace,

it is sometimes hard to see
the humans still on the ground.

If even partially true for you,
consider reading
this book again.

My thoughts

My feelings

My beliefs

My experience

Only humans express gratitude.

If you don't,
then what are you?

My thoughts

My feelings

My beliefs

My experience

at first light,

gratitude.

at lights out,

gratitude.

Fill your day with

possibilities.

Remember the endpoints.

My thoughts

My feelings

My beliefs

My experience

There is a song

in your heart.

are you willing to dance to it?

My thoughts

My feelings

My beliefs

My experience

Hold someone

when

they die.

My thoughts

My feelings

My beliefs

My experience

Find someone

to hold you

when you die.

My thoughts

My feelings

My beliefs

My experience

Celebrate being human.

Practice gratitude.

My thoughts

My feelings

My beliefs

My experience

The Power of Sharing

I am full of thanks and gratitude that you have reached this point in *Handbooks for Humans, Volume 1*.

Perhaps it seems like an ending for some of you, but my deepest wish, whether or not you have done some work on your thoughts, beliefs, feelings, and experience, is that as you reach this point of surveying these guidelines, you can see, feel, and think of it as more of a new beginning.

...A beginning of making changes in the way you manage your life.

It does not matter if you make many or just a single change, or even if a seed is planted for a future transformation; I believe that this book has served its purpose.

The guidelines I have presented may seem obvious or even common sense to many, yet, from my own experience it is so easy to ignore or take them for granted. I have found that once I write them down, then read and reread them, it is easier to remember, and allow my thoughts and feelings to come together and process them in a new way. This has been a pleasant surprise to me, and I hope that you may also experience this in your own unique manner.

Many studies have shown when people write things down they create stronger memories. That is the reason that *Handbooks for Humans* is much more than just a little book of inspirational sayings. It is a workbook, where if you are willing to follow through and write down how each guideline lands for you, I suspect the impact of this book may have some longer lasting results to your life and effects on your relationships.

In one way, this is a book for personal growth, but personal growth cannot really occur in a vacuum. We all must be in relationship. If you do the work here, and you are willing to share it with others who are also willing to do the work, the power of your work will multiply. You may wonder by how much. That is totally up to you but make no mistake of the power of sharing. You will only know when you experience it, and even then, you may not be able to find the words to describe it.

On the following page there is a place for you to do some personal reflection and additional work on what you may have experienced so far.

I encourage you to keep going, keep growing, and each day become a better human. It is habit forming, and a good habit to have.

NOTES

I am grateful for

NOTES

What being human means to me

NOTES

My personal guidelines in being human include

NOTES

I want to share this handbook with

More Guideline Reflections

There are many more ways to reflect on the guidelines than just exploring your feelings, thoughts, beliefs and experiences. However you choose to explore them is the work that you will do to hopefully lead you to a new path.

Feel free to create your own methods for further reflection and then share your techniques too. To get started, here are a few additional ways, to explore these paths.

Have there been particular guidelines that specifically speak to you? Pick three to five that have the most impact for you. What plan have you made to work with them further?

For each guideline, how does it affect you positively or negatively? Was your response to the guideline immediate or did you find that it simmered and built over time? Where has that led you?

In what ways does any guideline trigger you? (If you prefer to skip it, that is OK.) If you are willing to further explore your reaction, what concerns you about where this may lead you?

Which of the following descriptions best convey your thoughts on how the guideline resonates with you?

- Too simple
- Too hard
- Too obvious
- Just right
- Not relevant
- Provides incentive to change
- Already have it nailed

Has a guideline reinforced a message that you have heard before, but not responded to? Has the message landed differently for you reading it in this handbook? How will the guideline inspire you to act or do something differently?

Which guidelines stood out for you the most as relevant to your present situation? How do they affect you in your present state?

Which guidelines would you like to aspire to? What is standing in your way? What is one step you can take to initiate the change you would like to see?

When sharing your responses with others, what more have you learned about them? What more have others learned about you? Change is not always easy and often must be proved by being consistent.

As you read through the guidelines, you may have noticed that although they were presented in no specific order, most fall into four different categories:

Personal Guidelines

Relationship Guidelines

Life Cycle Guidelines

Gratitude Guidelines

You may want to review and reflect on the guidelines with these categories in mind or perhaps even place them in new categories of your own making.

By looking at these categories, it can bring you to a new place for sharing and discussion on your thoughts and feeling, in a more structured manner.

I am excited to share with you plans for creating community groups where you can share these and also a course where I will facilitate webinars focused on each category. For more information please find and like the Handbooks for Humans Facebook page.

Books by Grace Anne Stevens

*No! Maybe? Yes!
Living My Truth*

*Musings on Living
Authentically*

Become Part of the Community

If you would like to be added to the interest list for *Handbooks for Humans*, please enter your address here:

https://mailchi.mp/515db485e4cf/handbooksforhumans

about the author

Grace Anne Stevens writes and speaks on living authentically.

After over forty years as an engineer and manager in the tech world, she returned to school and received her M.A. in Counselling Psychology at the age of 62. She has participated in and seen life from many sides.

In addition to *Handbook for Humans: Volume 1,* she has published two other books so far and looks forward to what the future may bring as she continues learning how to be a better human. From 2015 to 2017, she contributed a weekly column on living authentically to the *Huffington Post*.

In 2016 Amtrak selected Grace as one of their Writer's in Residence and New England Pride TV named her Person of the Year.

Made in the USA
Middletown, DE
21 December 2018